Sheila Kimono Style + Plus

Sheila Cliffe

シーラの着物スタイル ＋ プラス

シーラ・クリフ

かもめの本棚

はじめに

着物の美しさに心を奪われ、日本で暮らすようになって36年が過ぎました。私の生活はいつも着物とともにあります。1年365日ほぼ毎日のように着物を着ていますが、決して飽きることはありません。長方形の布を縫い合わせただけの着物はそのシンプルなシルエットゆえに、帯や半襟、帯締めなどとのコーディネートによって驚くほど違う表情を見せてくれます。想像の翼を広げることで、一枚の着物から無限大の着こなしができるといっても過言ではないでしょう。

私の着物コーディネートを皆さんに初めてお見せした『SHEILA KIMONO STYLE』から3年。今回は、「Elegant」「Antique」「Plain & Pattern」「Casual」の4つのカテゴリーに分けて紹介しています。とはいえ、ここにあるのは私だけの"シーラ・スタイル"です。ですからこれをそのまま真似するのではなく、そこからいくつかのヒントを得て、世界にたった一つの自分だけの着物スタイルを作り上げてください。

たんすの奥や博物館の中に丁寧に保存しておくだけでは、着物という日本の美しい文化を守り伝えていくことはできません。毎日の暮らしの中で着ていくことこそが、伝統を守り伝える道ではないでしょうか。私が考えるシーラ・スタイルとは、「楽しく着物を着ること」。出かける場所や相手のことに思いを巡らせ、どのような着物を着ていこうか、どんな組み合わせにしようかなどと考える時間はとても楽しく、心豊かな時間です。

いくつになっても、どんなときでも、おしゃれをする気持ちを忘れずに着物を思いきり楽しんでほしい。心からそう願っています。

Introduction

Over 36 years have passed since I lost my heart to the beauty of kimono, and started my life in Japan. My lifestyle is always with kimono. I wear it almost 365 days a year, but I never get tired of it. Even though it is just one long piece of cloth sewn together, coordination with the obi, collar, obijime etc. mean that this simple silhouette can produce a breathtaking number of coordinations. It is not an exaggeration to say that if you soar on the wings of your imagination, there is no limit to the stylish looks you can create with one kimono.

3 Years have passed since I first showed you my styles in "SHEILA KIMONO STYLE". This time I introduce outfits I have divided into 4 categories: Elegant, Antique, Plain and Pattern and Casual. It is all my own style. I don't think it is good just to copy it directly, but to pick up some pointers to help you to make your own style, that is individual and unique in the whole world.

If kimono are only stored in drawers or in museums, we cannot preserve and continue this beautiful Japanese culture to the next generation. It is important for keeping culture alive that it is a part of our daily lives, isn't it? The concept behind Sheila Style is to wear kimono joyfully. Thinking about the places you will go, and the people you will meet and planning the coordinations is a rich and fulfilling way to spend your time.

However old you are, and to whatever occasions you attend, I hope you will not forget to enjoy the stylish possibilities of dressing in kimono. This is my heartfelt wish.

Contents

Sheila's Friends

すてきな人に会うときや、すてきな場所に行くとき
には、ちょっぴり優雅で上品に装いたいものですよね。
でも特別な日だからといって堅苦しく考えなくてい
いの。もちろんTPOを考えることは必要ですが、な
によりも大切なのはおしゃれを楽しむ気持ちです。

When you are going to meet someone special, or
go to a lovely place, you want to wear something
a little bit sophisticated. But just because it is
special, you don't have to think of it as needing
stiff, formal wear. Thinking about formality is
important, of course, but it's more important to
turn up stylishly and have fun.

ちょっとおしゃれをして銀座に出かけました。普段は着物から選ぶことが多いのですが、この日最初に決めたのはバッグ。赤い鯉と黒の波模様がどこか和を連想させるデザインだけど、実はスコットランド製です。このバッグに合わせて、黒とアクセントカラーの赤を使った大人っぽいコーディネートにしました。洋風なカトレア柄がモダンな雰囲気の銀座にぴったりでしょ？

I wanted to look a little stylish for going out to Ginza. Usually I start with the kimono, but today I wanted to use this bag. The red carp in the waves look Japanese, but actually the bag is from a Scottish brand. To go with the bag I chose a black kimono with red accents in a sophisticated style. I thought the cattleya, a western looking flower, has a modern feeling. Don't you think it is perfect for Ginza?

帯のブルーは別として、残りはすべて着物に入っている色でコーディネート。宝石のようなイヤリングを付けて、全体的にフランスっぽい雰囲気にしてみました。ライラック色の訪問着に描かれているのはバラの花。陶器の帯留にもバラが手描きされています。実はこの帯留は私の母が持っていたブローチなんですよ。

With the exception of the blue lines in the obi, all the other colours I used are found in the kimono. Using fake diamond earrings, I tried to make an image of something French. On the lilac background of the homongi, the pattern is of painted roses. The obidome was a painted porcelain brooch which originally belonged to my mother.

ターコイズブルーと黒のバラ柄の御召は、光沢があるのでパーティーでもOK。バラのゴージャスなイメージに合わせて、クジャクの羽根が描かれた黒の帯を選びました。キーカラーはターコイズブルーとピンクと赤。洋服だったら絶対にピンクと赤は合わせないからちょっと迷ったけど、なんとなくもう一つだけ色を入れてもいいかなと思って決めました。

This shining turquoise and black rose patterned omeshi kimono is fine for parties. To go with the gorgeousness of the roses I chose a peacock feather, black obi. The key colours are turquoise, red and pink. In global dress I wouldn't put red and pink together, but I wanted to add another colour, and pink seemed to fit in well.

この黒留袖はパーティーに着て行こうと思って手に入れたの。でも、そのままで着るとやっぱり面白くない。だから着物の着丈を短めにして長襦袢の赤を出してみました。こうすると、裾の部分に描かれている着物の柄が見やすい位置になるんですよね。黒留袖というとフォーマルな場で着る印象があるけれど、それだけじゃもったいない。みんなにも黒留袖でもっと遊んでほしいと思っています。

I bought this kuro tomesode, black formal kimono, with the intention of wearing it to a party. But it wouldn't be interesting to just wear it in the regular way, so I tied it up much shorter, to show the red under kimono. Actually, by making it shorter, you can see the painted pattern much better. Of course these kimono have the image of formality but if they are only used for those occasions it is a shame. I would really like to see people getting out these kimono and thinking of new ways to enjoy them.

30年以上前からずっと愛用している着物です。ターコイズブルーの帯締をアクセントに、シンプルでモダンな装いにまとめました。着物も帯もバッグも柄模様。でも、すべて幾何学模様というか抽象的な柄だから、全体で見ると統一感が出ているでしょ？ 柄と柄を合わせるときには「花柄と花柄」のように、同じカテゴリーの中から選ぶと合わせやすいですよ。

I have loved this kimono for over thirty years. I have made an accent with the turquoise of the obijime, but it is a simple, modern style. The kimono, obi and bag all have different patterns, but they are all geometric, so I have the feeling that they compliment each other. Do you agree? When mixing different patterns together it is sometimes helpful to use the same type of pattern repeatedly.

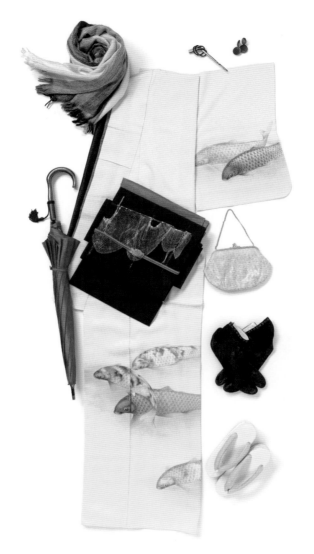

単衣の鯉の着物。鉛筆で描いているように見えるぐらい線が細かいの。限定された色しか使っていないところも、カッコいいと思っています。だからこの日は黒と白とグレーでまとめて、ポイントとして少しだけワインレッドを加えました。黒い帯に描かれているのは魚捕り用の網。帯留には木工細工の鯉。ストーリー性のあるこんな着こなしも着物だからできるんですよね。

This is an unlined kimono with a carp design. The lines are so fine that it looks like it is drawn with a pencil. I think the limited colour palette is very cool. I put it all together with black, white and grey, and for a special accent I added burgundy. The black obi has a pattern of fishing nets. A carved wooden carp obidome swims on the obi. It is only in kimono that one can coordinate with this sense of a story happening.

雨の夜のお散歩にはキラキラ光る素材でおしゃれに華やかに。エレガントでポップでしょ？
帯揚と頭飾りは洋装生地屋さんで探した布で作りました。気に入った布を選んで適当な長さと
幅に切れば完成です。装いのアクセントに選んだのは飾り腰紐。浮世絵に描かれた女性から
インスピレーションを受けて考案した私のオリジナルです。

I made a bright and shiny outfit for walking in the rain at night. Elegant but pop? The obi
age, hair decorations and collar I made with cloth from a fabric store. I just picked the
cloth I liked, cut it to the right size, and job done! The other accent I chose is a kazari
koshihimo, decorative kimono tie. I took inspiration from women in ukiyoe prints and
created this original item.

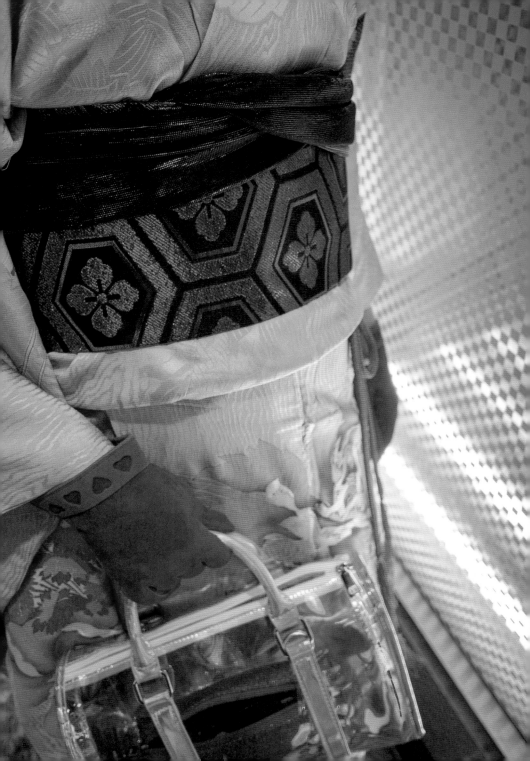

着物に使われている色だけでコーディネートしました。ほかの色は足さない、ある意味ではすごくオーソドックスな着こなしです。でも、どんなときでもちょっと手を加えるのが"シーラ流"。そこで、オリジナルの飾り腰紐で自分らしさを表現しました。美しい鳳凰が描かれた手描友禅の着物は私のお気に入りです。

For this outfit I used only colours that are in the kimono. Adding no extra colours, the look is very orthodox. I always like to add a bit of my personal style though. I decided to use my original, decorative kimono tie. There is a beautiful phoenix in hand-dyed yuzen on this kimono. It is one of my favourites.

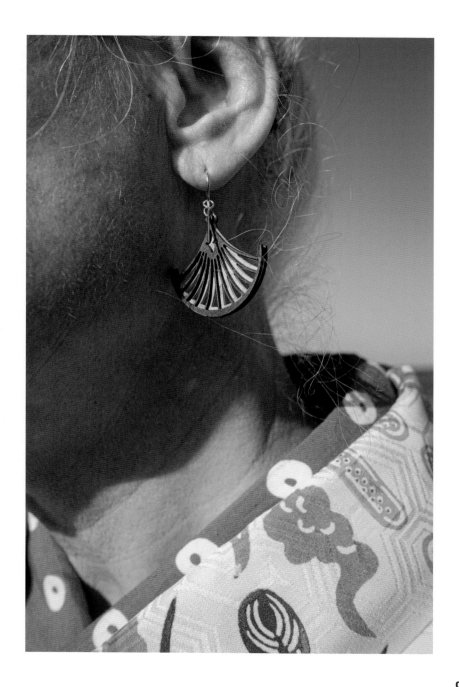

沖縄の紅型の着物。単衣で小紋の振袖という、ちょっと珍しい着物です。この着物にどんな帯をしたらいいのか迷いましたが、表がゴールド、裏がえんじの無地の帯を文庫結びにして合わせました。無地の帯にしたことで、着物の柄がよりいっそう引き立ったと思っています。

This kimono is Okinawan bingata dyeing. It is an unlined kimono with a komon, all-over pattern, so it is a rather unusual furisode. I was really undecided about what kind of obi to coordinate with this kimono, but in the end I went for a plain obi that was gold on the front and rust on the back, and tied it in a big bow. The result of not bringing in another pattern is to focus on the pattern on the kimono itself.

色留袖の上品でオーソドックスなコーディネートですが、飾り腰紐で自分らしさを出しました。濃い紫色がアクセントになっています。淡い色ばかりなのでポイントになるような色を入れたくて、この色を選びました。染めの着物のように見えるかもしれませんが、これは縫取。細かな模様がすべて「織り」で描かれている、とても手の込んだ着物です。

This is a relatively orthodox take on wearing an elegant iro tomesode, formal kimono. However I have given it my personal flavour by using a decorative kimono tie. It is a deep purple colour. Everything was pastel so I chose this strong colour as an accent. This looks like a dyed kimono, but actually it is nuitori, which means all the flowers are woven into the kimono. It is a very time consuming and challenging technique.

Sheila's Friends

田邊慶昴 さん
（けいこう）
（東京手描友禅作家）

Tanabe Keikou
(Tokyo yuzen artisan)

　すてきな帯を締めている人だなと思って声をかけたら、自分の作品だと教えてくれたの。話し始めてほんの数秒で仲良くなっちゃった。それが始まり。友禅の道をずっと歩いてきた女性ですが、考え方が柔軟でとってもフレンドリー。一緒にトークショーや着付け体験などもやりました。今では家族ぐるみのお付き合い。2人の娘の成人式の振袖も作ってもらいました。花鳥風月に限らず、着る人の個性に合わせたユニークできれいな図案を提案してくれるし、年齢を重ねても新しいことにチャレンジし続けている。慶昴さんという人間が大好きだし、彼女の作品も大好き。お互いに応援し合う仲です。

Keikou and I became friends almost instantly, when I commented that the obi she was wearing was so beautiful, and she told me that she'd made it herself. That was our beginning. She has always walked the yuzen path, but she is a very friendly and open-minded teacher. We have done talk shows and dressing events together. Now she is almost family. She made furisode for my two daughters. She doesn't just make the traditional flowers, birds, and seasonal designs, but creates unusual and unique designs according to the customers' needs, and has not stopped challenging new ideas as she has grown older. I love Keikou as a person and as an artist. We really admire and support each other.

http://www.dentou-kougei.com/keikou/

→ p.32 （着物 Kimono）
　　p.140 （帯 Obi）

Sheila's Friends

2年前にとっても珍しい織りの反物に出合いました。表は黒く見えるんですね。でも実際には紺色でブドウの模様が織ってあって、裏地は市松模様。「丹後」と書いてあるだけで、誰の作品かわからなかったのですが、全く違う布みたいで面白くて。着物はいっぱいあるから迷ったけど、とっても気に入ったから結局は買いました。その後、仕事で丹後に行ったときに江原さんの工房を訪れたのですが、そこで私が買ったのと似ている反物を見せてもらったの。急いで私が仕立てた着物の写真を見せたら、なんと本人の作品！ ほんとにびっくりしちゃった。江原さんの反物からは新しい着物の風を感じます。

江原英則さん
（江原産業）

Ebara Hidenori
(Ebara Sangyo)

Two years ago I found a really unusual woven tanmono, a roll of kimono cloth, that I loved. The front looked black with a pattern of grapes on it, but it was actually dark blue, and the back was ichimatsu, a check. It said "Tango weaving" on it, but I had no idea who had made it. It looked like completely different material from the front and back, and I hesitated because I have so many kimono already, but in the end I bought it. Later I went to Tango and I visited Ebara Hidenori's workshop. I saw a tanmono that was very similar to mine, so I found a photograph of the kimono I had had made up from my cloth and it turned out that it came from his workshop. I was totally amazed. I feel a wind of change coming from his workshop.

https://ebara-sangyo.jp/

→ p.14, p.90（着物 Kimono）

アンティークの着物は自分らしく自由に遊べるから、
カジュアルなお出かけに着ていくことが多いですね。
大正や昭和の着物は、秩父や川越といった歴史の
あるレトロな町並みによく似合います。

Antique kimono can be freely styled, so I often
choose them for going out casually. Taisho or
Showa period kimono are great when going to
historical towns such as Chichibu or Kawagoe,
because they match the architecture of the
places.

小江戸・川越へのお出かけに選んだのは、色づかいと構図が大胆な梅の着物。着物に合わせて帯も梅。春のお出かけにぴったりだと思いませんか？　パッと見ると色をたくさん使っているように思えるけれど、そんなことはなくて全部着物の中にある色。黒のバッグで全体をキュッと引き締めています。帽子もかわいいでしょ？

I went out to have fun in Kawagoe, often called Koedo or little Edo. I wore this in-your-face, bright kimono with big plum blossoms on it. At a glance it looks like there are loads of colours here, but actually I only used the colours that were in the kimono. The black bag brings it all together, but the hat is also cute, isn't it?

アンティークの着物を探しに浅草へ。着物を着ているとお店の人が気軽に声をかけてくれるから、いろんな話ができるんです。昭和の着物だと思うのですが裏地がすごく派手な紫。そこで草履も紫の花柄にしました。

Off to Asakusa to look for antique kimono. If you wear one, the shop staff are always friendly and are happy to talk with you. I think this is a Showa period kimono, but the lining is an amazing bright purple. I matched that with my purple flowered zouri.

この着物と72ページの青い着物は、私が出演したテレビ番組を見た人からもらったものです。どんな方が、どのように着ていたものなのか、詳しくはわからないのですが大切にしてあったのは確か。草木染のように思えるので、それに合わせて藍染のスカーフを帯揚に使い、帯もナチュラルな色づかいのものを選びました。

This kimono, and the blue one (p.72) were given to me as a present by a viewer who watched me on television. I don't really know anything about the owner, but I know it was looked after carefully. The colour scheme looks almost like natural dyes, so I used an indigo-dyed scarf as an obiage, and an obi with natural looking, soft colours.

この着物大好き！ ものすごく派手でしょ。だから華やかで自由なコーディネートにしました。
着物にも帯にも牡丹と桜が描かれています。着物と帯を決めたら、なんとなくロマンチックな
感じがしたし、ちょうど色もぴったりだったので、草履ではなくパンプスに。アクセントに黒の
ビーズバッグを持ちました。

I love this kimono. Isn't it great? The kimono and obi have peonies and cherry
blossoms. Once I had decided on the kimono and obi it looked kind of romantic, and
the colours were just right, so I used these turquoise shoes instead of zouri. The black
bead bag is an extra, elegant accent.

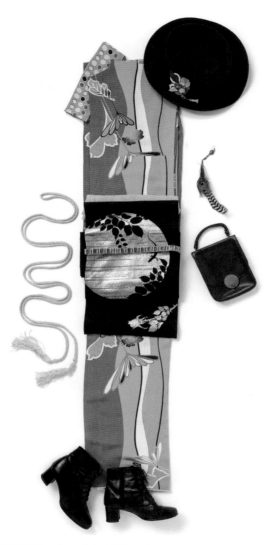

秋のお出かけの装いです。ちょっとわんぱくでボーイッシュな感じを出したかったから、髪を
三つ編みにしてブーツを履いて、片耳だけにイヤリング。大好きな帽子を被りました。帯に大
きなお月さまが描かれているでしょ。だから半襟と帯揚、飾り腰紐はお月さまと同じ黄色に。
半襟の水玉模様も満月を思わせます。

This is an autumn outfit. I wanted to look like a tomboy, so I put my hair in plaits
and wore black boots and one earring. I put on one of my favourite hats. The collar,
obiage and decorative kimono tie are the colour of the moon. The dots on the collar
also remind me of the moon.

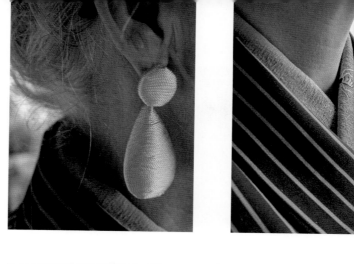

明治時代の散歩着だと思います。縞の御召に糸巻と絹糸、そして蚕と繭が刺繍されている。まさに"着物のストーリー"を語っている着物です。半襟にちょこんと姿を見せているのは蜘蛛。絹の糸も、蜘蛛の糸も、同じ糸でしょ。それでこの半襟にしました。

I think the kimono is from the Meiji period. It is a striped, omeshi sanpogi. It is actually telling the story of kimono with a moth, cocoon and threads. I am only showing a little bit of collar, but it shows a spider in its web. It is also making thread, which is why I wore this collar.

大正時代の終わりぐらいの古い着物です。着物の地模様をよく見ると、なんだか森の木々のように思えてきたので、真っ赤なポンセチアの飾りのついた帽子を被って、クリスマスをイメージしてみました。クリスマスシーズンのうきうきした気分に合わせて、遊び心たっぷりの足袋をチョイス。足元もコーディネートの大切な要素です。

This kimono is probably from the late Taisho period. The woven ground sort of looks like a pine forest, so I put it with a hat with a poinsettia decoration to make it like Christmas. I used black and red tabi to complete the playful Christmas themed look. The footwear is an important part of the outfit.

光をテーマにしたコーディネート。着物に描かれているのはシャンデリアか豪華な街灯です。着物の上に羽織ったコートは、おそらく着物をリメイクしたもの。羽織ではありません。ちょっと形が違います。着物自体はそれほどステキだとは思っていなかったけど、コーディネートするとびっくりするぐらいおしゃれになりました。

The theme of this outfit is light. The kimono has a gorgeous chandelier on it. The coat is probably made from an old kimono, it isn't a haori, it has a different construction. The kimono itself is not that special, but when it is coordinated, it looks surprisingly stylish.

ご近所さんに新年のご挨拶に行ったときのコーディネートです。帯に松と竹、着物には梅で"松竹梅"。お正月にぴったり。おめでたいでしょ？　白い足袋を選ぶ人が多いのかもしれませんが、私は黄色をチョイス。このほうが温かみもあって面白いと思うんです。

I paid my first New Year visit to my neighbour in this. The obi has pine and bamboo, and the kimono has plum, so it's perfect for New Year in Japan. Isn't it celebratory? Most people would choose white tabi, but I thought the yellow ones would give it more warmth, and they look fun.

ライムグリーンは私の大好きな色。この着物は金糸や銀糸、色糸で文様を織り上げた縫取御召に友禅を施した豪華な一枚です。着物が派手だから帯は黒。着物と同じ梅と竹が刺繍された名古屋帯です。今の人はこのような派手な着物をあまり着ないので残念。すごく楽しい気持ちになりますよ！

Limegreen is one of my favourite colours. This kimono has gold and silver threads woven into it. It is nuitori omeshi but it is extra lovely because it also has yuzen dyeing on top of it. Because it's so gorgeous already, I put it with a black obi. It has the same plum and bamboo patterns as the kimono. It is an embroidered Nagoya obi. It is a shame that people don't often wear such gorgeous kimono any more. It makes me feel really joyful to wear something so wonderful.

Sheila's Friends

柴田祐史さん

（柴田織物）

Shibata Yuji
(Shibata Orimono)

　金糸、銀糸、ラメ糸などで模様を縫い取ったぜいたくな「丹後縫取ちりめん」の訪問着や黒留袖で知られる工房ですが、私が注目しているのは男性用のおしゃれな着物。男性用というと無地とか縞模様が多いけど、柴田さんの着物はスネークスキンや、さびの付いた縞鋼鈑のデザインなど、モダンでスタイリッシュ。自分で作った着物をダンディーに着こなしている姿もカッコいい。海外ブランドや西陣のメーカーとコラボしたり、考え方も自由で新しいものを作りたいといつも思っている。会うたびに自分の作品について語ってくれます。男性の着物ファッションを引っ張っていく一人だと考えています。

Shibata Yuji is a maker of nuitori Tango chirimen, a very gorgeous kimono fabric using gold, silver and lame in the weft threads, which is used for the making of homongi and tomesode, formal wear. However, I became interested in his more modern and original menswear. Men's kimono tend to be plain or occasionally striped, but Shibata's kimono are snake skin or iron sheeting: modern and stylish designs. He looks cool and dandy wearing his own designs. He collaborates with overseas brands and makers in Nishijin Kyoto, and is always thinking about making something new. Whenever we meet he tells me about his work. He is one of the designers leading men's kimono fashion.

http://www.shibata-orimono.com/

→ p.82 （着物 Kimono）

Sheila's friends

るみさんが「Rumi Rock」として活動を
始める前から知っています。誰かが彼女の
浴衣を着ているのを見て、興味を持った
のがきっかけだったかな。伝統的な型染
の一種である注染の技術にこだわってい
るところが、面白いと思ったの。それと、
すごく使いやすくてキラキラした兵児帯
も好きです。るみさんのデザインはかわい
いだけじゃない。独特の世界観がある。
ばら銭で描かれたバラの花とか、江戸の
夜の町にいくつも浮かぶ提灯とか、大き
な海老とか金魚とか……。ちょっと不思
議な、独特のミステリアスな雰囲気のす
べてにストーリーがあって、なにか深く
考えているような図案なんです。

I have known Shibasaki Rumi since
before she branded herself Rumi Rock.
I think I met someone wearing one of
her yukata and that got me interested.
I was fascinated in the fact that she
was using a type of stencil dyeing,
chuusen zome, and I was also excited
by the really easy to tie, shiny, heko obi
that she developed. Her designs are
never just cute. There is always more
to them: A rose made out of barbed
wire, lanterns in an Edo night, a giant
goldfish or lobster. The uniquely strange
or mysterious designs are the result of
legends and stories, which really make
you think.

https://www.rumirock.com/

芝崎るみさん
(Rumi Rock)

Shibasaki Rumi
(Rumi Rock)

→ p.8, p.18, p.58 〔帯 Obi〕

Plain & Pattern

色無地や格子柄、幾何学模様は、四季を問わずに
自由に遊べる便利な着物です。色無地には白襟、
白足袋のイメージがありますが、私はもっとカラフ
ルに、帯や半襟、飾り腰紐などの小物で遊びたい。
ポップにおしゃれに。コーディネートの可能性は無限
大に広がります。

Plain, check or geometric designs are really
useful because you can wear them at any
season. Plain kimono have the image of going
with white collars and tabi, but I prefer to style
them with coloured collars and accessories and
to add a decorative kimono tie. If you enjoy the
pop nature of mixing and matching colours,
there are endless possibilities.

川越で秩父銘仙の反物を見つけて、1000円か2000円ぐらいで買いました。うちに帰って広げたら16メートル以上もあったの。それで単衣のカジュアルな振袖を作りました。昔はこのような、普段着としての振袖もあったらしいんですよね。一般的に振袖は未婚の若い女性の着物とされているのでフォーマルの場では着ませんが、振袖を着ると華やかな気分になるし、ほんとに楽しいの！

I found and bought a meisen bolt of cloth in Kawagoe for 1,000 or 2,000 yen. When I got home, I measured it and found over 16 metres of cloth. So I decided to make it up as an unlined, casual furisode, even though this cloth is really for ordinary wear. Apparently such casual furisode did exist once. Generally only young, unmarried women would wear a furisode, so I wouldn't wear it on a formal occasion, but furisode are bright and cheerful, so I really enjoy this one.

黒の色無地ですが、近づいて見ると地紋が浮き出てアクセントになっている。宝石や江戸切子のような地紋です。裏地は鮮やかなピンク。この反物を買ったとき、黒の着物にちょっとだけピンクの線が見えたらおしゃれだなと思って選びました。カッコいいでしょ。

This is a plain, black kimono but when you look carefully you can see the pattern in the weave. The pattern is like jewels or cut glass. I chose the bright pink for the lining. When I got the bolt I thought that black with a very fine accent of pink would be a great combination. It looks cool, doesn't it?

私の好きなモスグリーンの色無地。縁起のいい青海波の地紋が入っています。この着物は、なんといっても裏地がステキ。隠れているところに柄を入れちゃう。日本ならではのチラリズムですよね。裏地に紫がちょっと入っていたので、コーディネートのもう一つの色は紫にしました。

I love the moss green of this plain kimono. It has a wave pattern in the weave. The lining of the kimono is really attractive. The pattern is all in a hidden place. It's that Japanese fascination with just having a small glimpse of something. There is purple in the pattern, so I decided to use purple for the accessories to this kimono.

ミントグリーンの色無地に、ピンクの飾り腰紐と帯揚。好きな色ばかりです。そのままだと
ちょっと物足りない感じがしたから、つまみかんざしを髪に。凝ったヘアスタイルにしなくても、
頭にちょっと何か足すだけでおしゃれになります。

I enjoy this mint green, plain kimono. The obiage and decorative kimono tie are pink.
Actually I love all these colours. I thought it needed something a little extra, so I put
the kanzashi in my hair. Even if the hair style is not special, you can make it look great
by adding an accessory like this.

表面と裏面の柄が全く違う両面織りの丹後産の反物。「この布、素晴らしい！」と思って手に入れました。友人の慶子さん（※東京手描友禅作家の田邊慶昴さん）に見せたら、「裏地が見えないのはもったいないから、片身替わりに仕立てたらカッコいいんじゃない」と言われたの。それで、その言葉どおりに仕立ててもらいました。この着物は夏物ですが、ほんとにクール。いろんな意味でクール！

The weave on the front and back of this Tango made cloth are completely different. I just thought it was so amazing that I bought it. I showed it to my friend, the Tokyo yuzen artisan Tanabe Keikou, and she said it would be a shame not to see the back too. She suggested that it would be cool to sew it up as katamigawari, using half the front, and half the back. I followed her advice and used the front and back when having it sewn. It is a summer kimono, and I think it is really cool, in many ways!

このコーディネートのポイントは華やかな帯。色無地の着物がこの帯をいっそう引き立ててくれます。着物と羽織はもらい物。着なくなって、たんすで眠っていたものを私が譲り受けました。着物の寿命が延びるし、エコですよね。洋服だとサイズが合わなかったり、トレンドスタイルが変わってしまったりするから、そんなことはできません。着物の良さだと思います。

The main focus of this coordination is the colourful obi. You can really make an obi stand out by using a plain kimono. The kimono and haori were gifts. They were lying unused in someone's kimono chest, so I accepted them. They will be used longer and it's ecological. It's difficult to do that with regular clothing because of the size and changing shapes. It is much easier with kimono. That is one of its attractions.

銘仙の着物です。着物の柄の中にちょっとだけ黒も入っているから、アクセントに黒の半襟と手袋を選びました。実は、外出したときは帽子を被ってなかったの。でも、たまたま見つけた古着屋さんでこの帽子を発見！　今日のコーディネートにぴったりだと思って迷わず買っちゃいました。似合うでしょ？

This kimono is meisen. The design has a little black in it, and I made that the accent, using it for the collar and gloves. Truthfully, I didn't go out with the hat. I just found it by chance at a used clothing store and decided that it would be great for the shoot. It goes perfectly, doesn't it?

正直に言うと、黄色は今まであまり着たことがない色です。髪の毛が真っ白だから、私には似合わないと思っていました。でも思いきって着てみたら、太陽とか花の明るい感じがして好きになっちゃった。これまで着物を選ぶときには大好きなグリーンや紫、ターコイズ系の色に自然と目が行っていましたが、そこで立ち止まるとコーディネートも偏っちゃう。だから、いくつになっても新しいチャレンジをし続けたいと思うの。

To tell the truth, until now, I really haven't worn much yellow. I thought it wouldn't really work for me because of my white hair. But when I tried it, it reminded me of flowers blooming and the sun, so I have started to like it. I have naturally veered towards green, purple and turquoises, but just to stop there would be a bit biased. I want to keep challenging new ways of coordination, however old I get.

グリーン、ピンク、白のカラフルな重箱に合わせてカラフルなコーディネートにしました。お正月の遊びです。この着物は流水地紋の色無地。帯に描かれている黄色の花がアクセントになっています。

The green, pink and white was coordinated to go with this juubako, a food box. It was just some fun that we had at New Year. The kimono is plain but has flowing water in the weave. The bold yellow flower on the obi makes a nice accent.

秩父銘仙の着物です。子ども用ではないと思いますが、丈がちょっと短かったのでわざと短く着て、おしゃれな赤の長襦袢を裾から出しました。長襦袢と帯は花柄で統一。着物は市松模様で四角だから、草履と足袋は丸い水玉にしました。

This kimono is Chichibu meisen. I think it might be a child's kimono. It is way too short for me, so I purposely wore it short and used a colourful red nagajuban underneath. There are flowers in both the nagajuban and the obi. The kimono is a check so I used stripes and polka dots on the footwear.

Sheila's Friends

平山佳秀さん & 山本あさこさん
(Modern Antenna)

Hirayama Yoshihide and
Yamamoto Asako
(Modern Antenna)

平山さんと山本さんは、ロックバンドもやっているご夫婦。二人ともロックが好きで 60's のポップアートが好き。カラフルでグラフィックデザインが得意で、若い人にすごい人気です。彼らが芝崎るみさん（77 ページ参照）と一緒にポップアップ・ショップを開いていたときに知り合いました。平山さんは京都の伝統ある引染工房の息子さんですが、3Dグラフィックなどの仕事をしてから着物の世界に入った人。着こなし方もとっても自由で、パーカーにスニーカーでその上に着物を着る。ほんとに着物のハードルを下げているんですね。二人にとって着物はファッション。そこがすごくはっきりしているんです。

Hirayama Yoshihide and Yamamoto Asako are a couple that make kimono and also have a rock band. They love rock music and 60s pop art. Their strong graphic images are popular with young kimono wearers. They often do pop-up shops with Rumi Rock (p.77) and that is how I got to know them. Hirayama is the son of a traditional kimono dyer in Kyoto, but he went into 3D graphic design before going into the world of kimono making. Their way of wearing kimono is very casual with sneakers and hoodies underneath. They are bringing down the high hurdle of wearing kimono. For both of them, kimono is fashion. That comes across clearly in their work.

http://modernantenna.com/

→ p.116（帯 Obi）

Sheila's Friends

織物の産地として古くから栄えてきた群馬の桐生で、伝統工芸品の桐生織と桐生絞の着物や帯を創作している泉さん。生地から絞りまで、すべて自分の工房で制作しています。私が愛用しているのは、埼玉・秩父産の蚕を使って織り上げた「風通御召（ふうつうおめし）」。NPO法人「川越きもの散歩」が企画して商品化したもので、全部、日本で生まれ育った蚕の絹です。薄い紫やピンク、ベージュなど、すごく淡い色のグラデーションの着物で、光沢があって上品なところが気に入っています。伝統産業ですが、彼はちょっとひと味違うものも作ろうとしている。実はまだ1回しか本人と会ったことがないのですが、気になる存在です。

泉 太郎さん
（泉織物）

Izumi Taro
(Izumi Orimono)

Izumi Taro is making the traditional Kiryu weaving and Kiryu shibori, (tie-dyeing) which has made Kiryu town a thriving textile centre from ancient times. Izumi Taro is doing every process from weaving the cloth to the tie-dyeing. The kimono in this book, which I love, is made using silk from silk worms bred and grown in Chichibu, Saitama. It is called futsuuomeshi. It was made as a part of a project organized by Saitama Kimono Walking group NPO, which ordered kimono made from real, grown in Japan, silk. It is pale purple, pink and beige etc. and has pastel gradations in the colour, but it also has a beautiful and elegant sheen, which I am very fond of. I love Izumi's slightly original take on very traditional work. I have actually only met him once, but I am very impressed by him and his work.

https://izumi-orimono.co.jp/

→ p.132 (着物 Kimono)

紬や絣、木綿の着物は地味で落ち着いたイメージ
があるかもしれませんが、私はそうは思いません。
普段着のストリートウェアだからルールがないの。
だからアイデア次第で自分らしい楽しいコーディ
ネートができるのです。

I think tsumugi, kasuri and cotton kimono have a
rather dull image, but I don't feel that way. As
regular street wear there really aren't strict rules.
You can bring all your ideas and imagination to
making these kimono into interesting ensembles.

着物を短く着て、銘仙柄のおしゃれな靴下を履きました。モダンガールのイメージです。着物も半襟も帯も靴下も、みんな柄。でも、どれも写実的ではなく図案化された柄を選んで全体の統一感を出しました。

I wore this kimono short, with meisen patterned socks. I wanted to make a modern girl image. The kimono, obi, collar and socks are all patterned. However, they are all rather geometric patterns, so this draws them all together.

私の故郷イギリスをイメージしたコーディネート。着物は洋服の生地屋さんで探した布で作ってもらいました。裏地もカッコいいでしょ？　工場の夜景が描かれています。イギリスといえばロック！　髪飾りは本物のレコードです。

Here I made the image of my home country, England. I searched for the kimono cloth in a fabric shop. The lining is pretty cool, don't you think? It's a print of factories. When I think of England, I think of rock music. I'm using a real record as a hair accessory.

とてもカジュアルな黒とえんじの縞紬の着物。龍の刺繍が入った黒い帯と合わせて、少し上品な雰囲気にしました。首に巻いたのは藍染のスカーフ。帯揚に使ったり、バッグに結んだり、スカーフはいろんな使い方ができます。

This is a very casual rust and black, striped tsumugi. I put it with a black, dragon obi with knotted embroidery to make it a little more stylish. I used an indigo-dyed scarf around my neck. It can go around the bag or even be used as an obiage. There are many ways to use scarves.

袖が丸くて丈がちょっと短いから、これはたぶん100年ぐらい前の子ども用の着物だと思います。いつもは3つか4つの色でコーディネートしますが、この着物にはたくさんの色が入っている。だから、ある意味ではすごく合わせやすいんです。今回は黄色の帯を締めましたが、緑や青の帯でもいいと思います。

The sleeves of this kimono are rounded and rather short. I think this kimono is about a hundred year old, girl's kimono. I usually stick with 3 or 4 colours, but this kimono has many colours in it. Actually it is pretty easy to coordinate. This time I put a yellow obi with it, but I think a green or blue one would work as well.

125

私は普段から着物で自転車に乗るけれど、スケートだってしちゃいます。この日のお出かけに選んだのは結城紬。すごく暖かいので冬の時期によく着ます。着物が地味な色なので、帯は華やかな紅型の帯。それでもまだ少し物足りなかったので、黄色の飾り腰紐をしました。

I often ride a bike in kimono, but this time I tried skating. I went out in a Yuki tsumugi. It is a really warm fabric, so very suitable for winter, and I wear it quite a lot in that season. The kimono is quite dark, so I have brightened it up with a bingata obi. It still didn't seem too fun, so I added a decorative kimono tie to it.

秩父銘仙を着て秩父にお出かけしました。帯は 114 〜 115 ページでも使った帯。コーディネートのイメージはモダンガールです。軽快なイメージを出したくて、長襦袢の代わりに白いシャツを着て黒のブーツを履きました。

I wore Chichibu meisen when I went to Chichibu. I used the same obi that I used in p.114-115. It is the image of a modern girl, and I wanted it to look light, so I used a shirt underneath instead of a nagajuban.

カジュアルだけどすごくエレガントな御召の着物。帯合わせはちょっと迷いました。紫の帯でもいいかなと思ったけど、それだとちょっと濃すぎて着物の淡い色の良さがなくなってしまう。そこで、帯もストールも淡いピンキーベージュに。帯締だけを濃い色にしてきりりと引き締めました。

This is a casual but very elegant omeshi kimono. I had a hard time deciding on an obi. I thought purple would be good, but when I tried, it looked too strong and dark and the subtly of the pastel colours was lost. So I chose soft, pinky beige for the shawl and obi. I used a dark purple accent with the obijime to pull it together.

久米島紬の着物に博多帯、羽織は大島紬と、地方色豊かな織物でまとめたコーディネートです。紬や絣は少し地味なイメージがあるかもしれませんが、そんなことはありません。紬も絣もとってもきれい。楽しい装いができます。

This outfit is a Kumejima kimono, a Hakata obi and an Oshima haori. It is made up of many different area's weaving. Tsumugi and kasuri have a rather dull image I think, but they don't have to be. They can be coordinated in a fun way.

細い麻糸で織られた近江縮の夏用着物です。半襟や帯締、バッグや帽子などの小物類も着物と同じ色にしてみました。縮はさらっとした着心地で涼しいから夏のお出かけにぴったりです。

This is summer linen, Omi chijimi. I have used the same colours in the collar, obijime, bag, and hat. Chijimi is a cool fabric and perfect for going out in summer.

パッと見るとすごくモダンな染紬ですが、琵琶や日本の伝統的な柄が描かれている。色と柄で遊んでいる感じがする楽しい着物です。帯も新しいものですが、描かれているのは江戸時代の妖怪。古いものと新しいもの、時代の融合と進化をイメージしたコーディネートです。

At a casual glance this looks like a very modern, dyed tsumugi, but if you look closely you can find a biwa and other very old Japanese designs in the pattern. The artisan has really played with the patterns and colours. The obi is new but the designs are apparitions and ghosts from the Edo period. It is a fusion of old and new, and this creates evolution in kimono.

Kimono Style Q&A

Q1

毎日のコーディネートは
どうやって決めているのですか?

How do you decide
what you will wear every day?

AI

どんな場所で、誰に会うのか。着物を選ぶときには、
とにかく相手のことを考えるところから始めます。
それと、どんな印象を相手に与えたいのかを考えるこ
とも大事。頭の中でイメージを固めてから2枚、3枚
と着物を出しては眺め、それに合う帯や半襟をじっく
りと時間をかけて選びます。だから前の晩にコーディ
ネートすることが多いですね。何を着て行こうかと悩
むのも着物の楽しみです。

The first thing I think about is who I am
going to meet, and then where I am going
to meet them. Then its also important to
think about the impression I want to create
for this person. I make the image in my head
and then get out two or three kimono and
then try several obi and collars with them. I
take my time and enjoy this process. I
usually start getting ready the night before.
Considering what to wear and thinking
about that is one of the joys of kimono.

Kimono Style Q&A

Q2

着物と帯の組み合わせに悩みます。

I am confused about what obi to put with each kimono.

A2

決まりはありませんが、いくつかのパターンはあります。例えば「波と船」「魚と網」のように、着物と帯の柄にストーリー性を持たせると面白いですよね。花柄と花柄、幾何学模様と幾何学模様など、同じカテゴリーの柄を選ぶのもいいでしょう。着物に入っている色の中からどれか1色を選ぶ、反対色を選ぶ、色の濃淡をつけるなど、色に着目して帯を選ぶのもいいと思います。私は普段、着物を決めてから帯を選びますが、例外もあります。それは個性的な柄の帯。この場合、着物がキャンバスで帯は絵画。だから色無地の着物を選びます。

There aren't any strict rules, but there are some guidelines that can help. For example, waves and a ship, fish and a net, so telling a story with the kimono and obi. It's really interesting. It's also good to use similar types of patterns, plants and plants or geometric designs. It is possible to choose opposite colours for the kimono and obi, or also choose a lighter or darker version of the same colour.

Kimono Style Q&A

Q3

襟元のおしゃれが苦手です。
半襟の選び方を教えてください。

I'm not good at using collars.
Please tell me how to choose good
collars.

A3

半襟は帯と着物の合わせ方に似ています。着物の色と合わせたり、着物の柄と同じモチーフでそろえたり。「半襟だから白」といった固定観念に縛られるのではなく、コーディネートのイメージを優先し、それを完成させるためにはどんな色や柄が欲しいのか？　自分の頭で考えてください。私は合わせたい色や柄があれば、手拭いやスカーフ、洋服や古い着物の生地など何でも半襟として使っています。

Choosing a collar is a bit like choosing an obi. I choose a similar colour to the kimono, or a pattern that is in the kimono. You don't need to think that collars should be white. Put the priority on completing the outfit and add whatever collar does that best. Think about it carefully. When I'm coordinating, it could be a scarf, cloth from a fabric store, a piece of old kimono, anything can become a collar.

Q4

たんすに眠っている着物を
カッコよく着こなすコツは？

How do you use the kimono lying
in the kimono chest in a stylish way?

A4

ちょっと時代遅れかなと思う着物でも、イアリングやバッグ、半襟や帯などのコーディネート次第で生まれ変わります。今の人は柄模様の洋服をあまり選ばないから、着物の柄はかえって新鮮に映るはず。色無地の着物には、色付きの半襟や足袋を合わせるのもおすすめです。せっかくの着物がたんすに眠ったままなんてもったいない。とにかくチャレンジしてみて！

Even if you think the kimono lying in the kimono chest at home are a little out of date, they can easily be made fashionable with the use of earrings and bags, and using collars and an obi. They can really be reborn. Nowadays people don't wear a lot of patterned items, so the patterns on kimono can look really fresh. I recommend using plain coloured kimono with coloured collars and tabi. It is a pity to leave them unused, so let's get them out and try!

Kimono Style Q&A

Q5

シーラさんみたいにすてきに着こなせる
自信がありません。

I don't have the confidence to wear
kimono stylishly like you do.

A5

"シーラっぽく"ではなく、自分らしく着こなしてほしいですね。おしゃれになるかどうかなんて、やってみないとわかりません。太っていてもやせていても、身長が高くても低くても、いろんな体形に対応してくれるのが着物のいいところ。「コーディネートのアイデアはどこから来るのですか?」とよく聞かれますが、全部、私の頭の中から来るの。ファッションには想像力が大事。一生懸命考えたら、きっといいアイデアが出てくるはずです。

I don't want you to just copy me, but to find your own style, and wear it your way. You will never find it out if you don't try. If you are fat or thin, tall or short, it is one of the advantages of kimono that it makes you look nice. People ask me where I get my ideas for coordination, but they are all inside my own head. Inspiration is important for fashion. If you think hard, something will emerge for you.

Kimono Style Q&A

Q6

明るい色にも挑戦してみたいけれど、
年齢を考えると実行に移せません。

I want to try bright colours,
but I feel too old for them,
so I don't try.

A6

年を取ったら地味にしなきゃいけないなんて、そんなこと誰が決めたの？　私は絶対に反対です。明るい色だってどんどん着て楽しめばいいの。色で失敗しないためのコツは、自分の好きな色を選ぶこと。だって好きな色を着ると幸せな気持ちになれるでしょう。おしゃれも人生も、いつまでも楽しみましょう！

Who decided that you have to be dull as you get older? I am completely against this idea. I think it's fun to go on wearing bright colours. The key to not making mistakes with colour, is to choose colours you like. Of course, you will feel happy when you are wearing colours that you like. We should enjoy our fashion all through our lives.

おわりに

　着物について語るとき、私の心の中にはいつも "Fashion is a Journey" という言葉が浮かんできます。ファッションとは長い旅路。生きている文化だからどこまでも終わりはありません。完成形はないのです。だからこそ私は冒険心を持って、変化を恐れずに新しい着物スタイルに挑戦していきたい。そんな気持ちを常に抱いています。ですから、『Sheila Kimono Style Plus』と名づけたこの写真集は私の旅（成長）の記録でもあります。

　本書で紹介した着物スタイルは、私と同じく着物を心から愛するニコルと一緒に2年間かけて撮影しました。大学院で着物文化を学ぶためにエクアドルから日本へ来た彼女は、努力を惜しまない頑張り屋さんです。豊かなセンスと器用な手先を生かして、常にベストな撮影ができるようにサポートしてくれました。心からお礼を言います。ニコルは2年間の留学期間を終えて故郷に戻りましたが、今後は日本で得た知識や経験を生かして、エクアドルと日本の架け橋になってくれることを願っています。

　私にとって、ファッションは自分自身を最も自由に表現できるもの。和装のルールを踏まえながらもそれに縛られるのではなく、ファッションとしての着物の可能性を思う存分に追求したいと思うのです。大好きな着物を通じて多くの人と出会い、私の世界は広がりました。それにより着物との新たな付き合い方も見えてきました。今後は着物のデザインやコーディネートのアドバイスなど、新しい挑戦もしてみたいと思っています。これからも着物を愛し、その魅力を世界中の人に発信していく考えですので、引き続き応援よろしくお願いします。

シーラ・クリフ

Afterword

Whenever I talk about kimono, the idea in my mind that "Fashion is a Journey" always comes up. Fashion is a long journey. It is a living culture, so there is no final destination. It is never a completed project. I want to have an adventurous heart and not be afraid of always embracing change and challenging new kimono styles. I cling to this principle. That is why I offer to you "Sheila Kimono Style Plus". It is a record of the next step or challenge on my journey.

I shot the photographs for this collection over a period of 2 years, with another kimono lover, Nichole. She came from Ecuador to Japan to study for a masters in kimono culture, and put in tremendous effort at everything, so she would have no regrets. She used her fine sense and artistic skills to always support me with great images. I want to thank her from the bottom of my heart. After her 2 year course, she had to return to her own country, but I'm hoping that there she is continuing to use the knowledge and skills that she gained in Japan to become a cultural bridge between Ecuador and Japan.

For me, fashion is the easiest way to express myself. While staying aware of kimono related rules, I try not to be tied up in them, but to always fully explore the possibilities of kimono as fashion. Thanks to my beloved kimono I have met so many wonderful people and my world has become richer. This has helped me see a new relationship with kimono. Going forward I am interested in advising about designing and styling kimono. It will be a new challenge for me. In the future I will continue to love kimono, and to share its attractions with the world, so I humbly ask for your support in my kimono journey.

Sheila Cliffe

Sheila Cliffe （シーラ・クリフ）

1961年イギリス生まれ。着物研究家。十文字学園女子大学名誉教授。リーズ大学大学院博士課程修了。大学で英語と着物文化を教える傍ら、国内外で着物展覧会やファッションショーの企画・プロデュースなど多彩な活動を展開。2002年に民族衣裳文化普及協会「きもの文化普及賞」を受賞。17年にはクリエーターとして注目を集める Akira Times 初の写真集『KIMONO times』（リブロアルテ）の出版サポートに携わる。著書に『日本のことを英語で話そう』（中経出版）、『The Social Life of Kimono』（Bloomsbury Academic）。18年に刊行した自身初の写真集『SHEILA KIMONO STYLE』（東海教育研究所）では、古着やアンティークを中心とした私服の着物コーディネートを紹介し反響を呼ぶ。以降、「丹後ちりめん創業300年」のアンバサダーをはじめ、テレビや新聞、雑誌などのメディアに多数出演しているほか、講演会やトークイベント、ワークショップを行うなど、活動の幅をさらに広げている。

Sheila Cliffe

Sheila Cliffe was born in England in 1961. She is professor emerita of Jumonji University. She has a Ph.D. from the University of Leeds. At her university she taught English and Kimono Culture, and has planned kimono exhibitions, events and fashion shows both in and out of Japan. In 2002 she was awarded the Kimono Culture Spreading Award by The Cultural Foundation for Preserving the National Costume of Japan. She supported the publication of creator Akira Times "Kimono times" Libro Arte in 2017, She wrote "Explaining Japan in easy English" Chukei Publishing, and "The Social Life of Kimono" Bloomsbury Academic. In her own style book "SHEILA KIMONO STYLE" Tokai Education Research Institute, she used mainly antique and used kimono styling and coordination and it was well received. Recently her influence is expanding as she was chosen as the "Tango Chirimen 300 Year Anniversary Ambassador" and has appeared on numerous TV programs and in media outlets. In addition she does speeches, talk events and workshops.

撮影 Photographer

Nichole Fiorentino （ニコル・フィオレンティーノ）

1992年エクアドルの首都キト生まれ。グラフィックデザインを学び、2017年から2018年まで広告の仕事に携わる。2015年から着物と出会いコレクションを始める。19年から2年間、文部科学省の奨学金を得て東京・文化学園大学の大学院修士課程に留学。カジュアルな着物文化に関する研究を進めるとともに、日本滞在中は友禅染や茶道を学ぶ。現在はキトに在住してエクアドルの人々に日本の文化を紹介している。

Nichole Fiorentino

Nichole Fiorentino was born in Quito, Ecuador in 1992. She studied graphic design and worked in advertising from 2017 to 2018. She has worn and collected kimono since 2015. For two years from 2019, She was granted the MEXT scholarship to study for a master's degree at Bunka Gakuen University in Tokyo, where she researched casual kimono culture. During her stay in Japan, she studied Yuzen dyeing and tea ceremony. Currently she resides in Quito, and shares Japanese culture in Ecuador.

Sheila Kimono Style Plus
シーラの着物スタイル プラス

2021 年 11 月 1 日　第 1 刷発行

著　者	シーラ・クリフ　Sheila Cliffe
撮　影	ニコル・フィオレンティーノ　Nichole Fiorentino
発行者	原田邦彦
発行所	東海教育研究所 〒160-0023　東京都新宿区西新宿 7-4-3　升本ビル 電話 03-3227-3700　ファクス 03-3227-3701 eigyo@tokaiedu.co.jp
印刷・製本	株式会社シナノパブリッシングプレス
装丁・本文デザイン	稲葉奏子
撮影協力	白根美恵（物撮）

© Sheila Cliffe 2021 ／ Printed in Japan
ISBN978-4-924523-24-1 C0077